Shyness

Written By

Table of Contents

Introduction

Shyness is a common problem faced by many people around the world. It is a common condition whereas the person who is shy feels unsure about putting themselves out there in social situations. It is commonly seen in young children, teens as well as adults who find it hard to interact with people and situations.

If you are shy there is nothing to be afraid of. Everyone is shy about something or another it is just how we deal with it that makes a difference. Shyness is something that can be overcome and for most people overcome fairly easily.

Throughout the pages of this book we will be exploring shyness and how people act and react to certain situations. We will explore the causes of shyness and ways to handle certain situations. It is the hope of the author that when the reader finished this book they will have a better understanding of shyness, what causes it and how they can adapt to become more confident.

Throughout the book we will be giving you tips, tricks and saying that will help you to overcome shyness and build up your confidence so that you will never be shy again.

Before we continue I just wanted to say one thing to my loyal readers, if you suffer from shyness don't be ashamed. It is a common phobia that everyone has. I had it when I was a kid and just until about two years ago I was shy when it came to talking to people. After reflecting on my life experiences and structuring myself through the tips that I will show you through the book I overcame being shy and now stand before you able to share my story as well as write this book so that you can benefit from my journey.

If you have ever felt that this is something that you couldn't overcome don't think like that anymore. Read through the pages of this book and apply what is taught to you.

Shyness can be overcome. Let's take the journey together.

Chapter One

Everyone is shy about sometime or has been shy at a point in their life. There are many reasons and or forms of shyness that someone can be afflicted with. Some are brought on by the fear or rejection and others are brought on by traumas from an event in their past. If you suffer from shyness there is help out here in the form of social groups, counseling and for extreme situations medication.

In this chapter we will explore some of the reasons someone may feel shy and then in future chapters we will go into greater details and give examples and stories that hopefully be motivational and inspirational to you in your recovery from this infliction.

What Is Shyness

Shyness is an emotion similar to love, hate, greed, fear and many others. When someone is shy it is a result of their emotional state trying to adjust to new people and situations. People who are shy are not bad people. Even though their actions may present them as being standoffish, or unfriendly people who are shy just have a tendency to take their time to warm up to new people, situations and events that don't fall within their comfort zone.

Shyness usually starts off when you are a kid. You are usually thrown into new and unfamiliar situations such as the first day of school, summer camp, groups or social clubs or anything that introduces the shy person to unfamiliar or uncomfortable situations.

A person who is shy will usually sit away from others or close to someone that they know or are familiar with. The shy individual will watch carefully the interactions of those at the gathering. They will see who they talk to, what they do, how they interact and who will best fit their personalities.

When someone is shy they will exhibit some common social or physical signs. Some of these will include sitting in the corner or away from others, they will display redness or a blushing of the face and hands. They will become fidgety and try to keep their hands busy and eye contact away from others.

How Shy People React To Situations And Events

Similar to other phobias and conditions shyness comes in several forms of severity. These levels include mild, medium and intense. Depending on the person's situation and ability to cope with new events the person may begin with a lower form of shyness and move upwards to the more severe or vice versa.

Someone who in on the mild side of shyness may just need a few minutes to adjust to situations and new people. These people can quickly assess the situation and move out of their shyness phase and quickly feel comfortable and begin to interact on a normal social level.

Someone who is mildly shy may take time to warm up to the situation. Sometimes they will need a friend to talk to in order to get out of their shell. They may need to be introduced to another person who by someone familiar and casually be brought into the conversation.

Those who have an intense phobia when it comes to shyness may take a long time to come out of their shell and become social. These people will force themselves into these situations trying to fit in and be a part of life but for most the longing for the familiar and comfortable is a constant presence in their minds. People who have the intense level of shyness often can become loners, shut-ins and worse. Without treatment or perhaps medication those who have an intense level of shyness can create debilitating conditions that will lead to a loss of life's enjoyments. If you or someone who has the intense form of shyness phobia you need to talk to someone and seek help in order to reestablish a semi-normal form of life.

Reacting To New Things

One of the first things that relate to shyness is the fact that people don't know how to react or act in certain situations. If you are a newcomer to a group or a club you may not be fully aware of all the policies, procedures, temperaments and goings on that occur in that situation. As a result you will usually stand back and assess the situation and find out what's what. Being the new person in the situation you will not know everyone involved and may be shy on what to say or what to do when approached by someone of authority or long standing in the group.

Another form of shyness comes when you are put on the spot in these situations and may be asked to talk about yourself or your problems. Being caught unaware of the situation you may hold back for a moment and think about what to say, what to do or how to act.

These types of situations are normal and shouldn't result in shyness activity for an extended period of time. When presented with these situations you will want to quickly gather your thoughts and emotions and face the situation head on with confidence.

In The Next Chapter

In the next chapter we will start at the heart of when shyness begins. For most of us this means our childhood. We will explore all aspects of shyness when it relates to being a child as well as things you can do as a parent to help encouraging shyness, having others encourage shyness as well as many other factors and treatments.

Don't be shy, visit us in the next chapter.

Chapter Two

When we are children we don't know all of the rules, regulation and how things are supposed to happen. Also as children we aren't really exposed to a lot of contact with other people. From birth we are usually only dealt with by our parents. Some of us may have brothers and sisters, grandparents, aunts and uncles and other family members that come in and out of our lives on a sporadic or semi-regular basis but that is not always the case.

As a result of this sheltered society that we live in as children we don't really have the opportunity to go out there and learn not to be shy. We are used to the familiar and anything other than that is alien to us. In this chapter we will explore several aspects of shyness and the mindset of not only the child but the parent as well. We will explore several areas that are controversial as well as areas that you might not think of that may result in the shyness of a child.

Heredity or Our Genes

In recent years it has been discussed by people in the scientific community that our genetic makeup contributes to our shyness and shyness activities. It is claimed by some scientists that we may have a shyness gene that is passed on from generation to generation.

Now none of this has been proven as of yet but wouldn't it be interesting to know that shyness is a genetic physiological occurrence. If this is true wouldn't it be interesting to see a drug or pill come out on the market that all you had to do was take it and you would become Don Wan.

On a serious note though, if you really sit back and think about it this really isn't farfetched. Shyness may not fall into a heredity issue or behavior but perhaps it is possible that there is a genetic or physiological aspect to shyness that can be altered at the physical level.

Here is an example. What happens when someone takes drugs or alcohol? For most of us it plays with our moods and emotions. These foreign chemicals interact with the chemicals in our bodies and alter our moods, behavior and actions.

Now I am not saying that shyness will someday be cured by a pill or that if you are shy that you need to start taking drugs and alcohol. What I am saying is that there may be more to this theory than just smoke. It will just take time to see where the science goes with it.

Inconsistent Parenting

Now it is time to get into the parents. Yes I know blame mom and dad for everything. Well no that isn't what I am doing. The fact is that like I stated in the first section that the parents are usually the first social contact a child will have. The parents set the tone for behavior, mannerisms and the mental health of a child. In general when a child is shown love they show love in return. When hey show hatred they show hatred in return. When they are told things are wrong or shouldn't be done that way subconsciously they become self-conscious and as a result shyness or unassertiveness soon follows.

Inconsistent parenting comes into play when you have one parent usually the mother but not always, taking the stern hand approach. This parent is usually the primary parent who is around the child all day long. They feed the child, bathes the child, clothes them as well as sees to their day today activities. As a result they are the biggest influence on the child.

The secondary parent is usually the father. In most cases but not always he is the bread winner. He goes out and makes the money to support the family. So for most of the day he is not in the life of the child. The child may see him first thing in the morning and then again at night before hey go to sleep. Then the father may be around on the weekends but even then he may be working on areas of the house or yard. As a result he is considered the inconsistent parent.

When it comes to parenting the father may take a leaner approach towards the rules and regulations. This is done because they feel guilty for not being there all the time. Then the opposite may be true. The father may be sterner or run a tight ship with rules and procedures within the home.

With this type of inconsistent parenting the child may become confused or unsure of how things work or are supposed to be. As a result the child may hide away to avoid the situations all together. If this behavior is not changed or altered it will follow them throughout their lives and result in a shyness phobia or social anxiety.

Lack of Parental Involvement

When you are growing up you need guidance. I know that we are all headstrong individuals who hate to ask for help or take advice from others but the reality is that we don't live alone on this planet and we need directions from our parents and role models.

When you have parents that don't take an interest in their children or their activities one of two things will happen. First that child will start to act out and do things to get attention or on the other side of the coin shy away and build their own world around them.

Lack of parenting comes into play when a parent is alone or also known as a single parent. The parent or parents work a lot of hours and as a result farm their children off to others to raise or deal with on a day to day basis. Or the parents are there but the thought of parenting is just too hard that they just lock themselves away and let the child for all intents and purposes raise themselves.

When you are a parent you need to take an active role in your child's life. You need to show your child that they are important not only to you but to themselves. You need to build self-esteem and morals within your child. You need to encourage them to get out there and do the best that they can do. It is a huge amazing world out there and the best way to prepare them for it is to be an active participant not a spectator.

Overprotective Parents

On the other side of the coin parents who are overprotective of their children will cause them to become lazy and unsure or unmotivated. When you are overprotective you have a tendency not to allow your children out of your sight. You jump every time your child sneezes or has a runny nose. You take them to the hospital every time they skin their knee or trip and fall.

Now you might be thinking that I am making this stuff up but sadly I am not. I know from firsthand experience that people baby their children. I had a friend who kept his son so sheltered from the world that one day I went with him to the mall and he wouldn't even get on the escalator.

You watch television shows all the time where you will have a five year old child breast feeding in a restaurant. If you were to type in overprotective parents into Google you would receive just like I did 1,580,000 results. That is a lot of results for a very big problem.

Signs To Look For To See If You Have An Overprotective Parent

#1 Going Through Your Stuff

When you have an overprotective parent they will generally go through your stuff and find anything that they think you should have or be harmful to you. This can be anything from a sharp piece of plastic to a paper clip. When you get older they will be looking for things such as rock and roll music, condoms, phone numbers to people of the opposite sex and who knows what else.

#2 Shadows You on the Internet or Your Phone

Now that we are in the digital age your parents will put on protective software to look for words like "Sex" "Drugs" or anything that they find inappropriate. They will start looking at your friends "if you have any" and see what they are saying to others. Once they find something or even the hint of something your phone, internet or whatever devil piece of technology you are using will be taken away from you.

#3 Back Seat Drivers When They Aren't Even In the Car

Driving as a teenager or young adult should be a rite of passage. For some kids it is a nightmare. Parents now have GPS and other technologies that they can use to monitor everything from your driving speed, time it takes you to apply the break as well as GPS to track your routes and traffic conditions. You may even be embarrassed by having signs put on your car saying that you are a new driver or maybe even worse "Baby on Board"

#4 "My Baby Is Getting Bullied"

With overprotective parents the thought of their child getting bullied or picked on in school is a constant through in their heads. Sometimes it gets so bad that kids will start getting picked on because of the actions of their parents.

#5 They Start To Make Problems Where None Exist

Overprotective parents will seek out problems where there are none. They will go to the parents of other children and tell them to stay away from their child or that the other parent's kids are a bad influence. And heaven forbid the child gets hurt or eats something that wasn't on the approved list of foods or drinks, you will never hear the end of it. So parents need to just chill out and let their kids be kids.

#6 Making Dating a Nightmare

Now when you do get older and want to start dating your parents will make it a living nightmare. You will never want to bring your date over to meet your parents because the nightmarish fear that they will embarrass you and bring out the photos of you as a kid in the bathtub are totally justified.

If by chance you do get a date or god forbid married, your parents might be sitting at the altar with a shotgun.

#7 They Will Treat Everyone Like A Sex Criminal Or Out With An Agenda

When you have overprotective parents they will look at everyone with a fine tooth comb. They will want to know everything about them before they even meet them and if for some reason something doesn't go right or they say the wrong thing you will never hear the end of it.

#8 You Will Have to Be Home an In Bed by a Specific Time

When you have overprotective parents you will need to be where you are supposed to be at all times. If you walk the wrong way home from school, are not at the bus stop at the exact second you should be or in bed at the same time even if it is a Saturday or non-school night you will be punished.

#9 Parents Will Use Punishments For Any Action They Seem Fit

The one thing with overprotective parents is that they have a need to be controlling. If for any reason you don't fit into the structure or rules they may hand down swift and severe punishments. Sometimes these punishments will be physical in nature such as a spanking or worse, but for the most part from my experiences the punishment is more fear based. The parents will use their authority to control the situation knocking down the person's self-esteem which will transfer into shyness or social anxiety disorder which is a more severe form of shyness.

#10 Sports And Social Activates Are Bad

The last one that we will talk about are sports and other social activities. When you have an overprotective parent they will find any reason to keep you away from playing sports or engaging in other social activities. The parents will fear that their child will get hurt, meet up with the wrong people start doing something that is not approved by the parent's belief system.

Without social interaction and the skills learned from these interactions people will not know how to deal with these situations when they are presented to them.

Lack of Experience in Social Situations

Like stated previously in the last section when someone has overprotective parents they have a tendency to not have the social interaction skills needed to be outgoing in social events such as parties, gathering and other events.

When someone is shy they are not exactly sure how to act or interact with others on a social basis. Someone who is shy will tend to find a comfort zone or a way of acting to make themselves feel included yet remain at a safe comfortable distance.

When someone is shy they may resort to nervous acting behaviors. They will move their eyes, fidget their fingers, have an oral fixation such as biting their fingernails or sucking on a straw or cherry stem.

Other actions they may exhibit are rubbing their hands together, swinging or moving their feet as well as avoiding eye contact. When it comes to kids and children in these situations they may not apply themselves to social activities, shy away from making friends or in extreme situations find ways to alienate themselves from other people resulting in solitude or antisocial behavior.

Modeling Or Learned Behavior

When we are children we pick up on things fairly quickly. We look at our parents, siblings and others who we come in contact with. I have a two year old granddaughter and over the past year she has grown and changed so much. Her actions and her temperament amazes me. She picks up on so many different things you have to go back in your mind and figure out where she learned it.

You also have to be careful on what you do and how you do it when you are around impressionable children. Every word you say, every action you make will be scrutinized by a child. For example, my stepdaughter smokes. She smokes in a way that her daughter will see it. So now you see my granddaughter imitating her smoking behavior.

The same goes with shyness. If your children see you being shy or acting in a shy manner they will pick up on that behavior and imitate it. When they get older they will continue to act in that manner not really knowing what it means or how it will affect them in the future.

Shyness May Lead To Problems in School

Shyness as a child is a problem that may affect you the rest of your life. For most children school is the first taste of social interaction that they will receive. When going to school they are thrown into a room with a least twelve to twenty other children their same or close to same age. They are subjected to rules and regulations brought on by the school system, they will be dealing with other children that have their own likes, beliefs and ways of doing things.

When a student is shy in school hey will have a tendency to be picked on or made fun of. Other children will think that they are strange and will force them into even more isolation. When you have a child that is not accepted or feels that they are unaccepted they will deviate themselves into their own world. As a result grades may slip, social growth will fall way and their entire educational experience will not be pleasant.

Low Self-Esteem or Negative Opinion of Oneself

One side effect of shyness in a child is the buildup of low self-esteem. When a child is shy hey will hide away and not put themselves out there to be judged. So when they do get some form of rejection they take it as a personal attack and won't try to put themselves out there again.

Others May See Shy Children As Stuck Up

Children, adults as well but mostly children have a high regards for themselves as individuals and don't like anything that distracts form or is different from themselves or their beliefs. Children feel that they are the center of the universe and don't feel that anyone should be different or just don't' understand how to react to someone that is different. So if you are shy and don't interact with them on their level they feel that you are stuck up or have an attitude. This can haunt you the entire cycle of your education at that school. The best thing to do is to let people know who you are and where you stand. You don't have to be going all out but learn to be comfortable with yourself and what you want.

Too Much Threatening, Teasing, or Criticism

To say it frankly and honestly kids are mean and like to pick on others because they are different. There is no easier way of saying it than that. When we are kids we have a tendency to pick on other because of the way they look, talk, act or just because we want to feel better about ourselves.

There is really no better way to explain it than that. When you are someone that is shy you won't take it as a thing that kids just do, you will take it on a more personal level and begin to crawl back into your shell or world of your own creation. You will begin to feel alone and that the world is against you. So as a result you will start to embrace your shy existence.

Threatening

When someone feels threatened they have a tendency to coil back and put up a defensive stance. When someone is threatened and shy they tend to ball up into a protective ball or shy away from the situation praying in their minds that it will go away. To the person who is doing the threatening they begin to feel even more power and know that they have found a suitable target so the threatening will continue on a continuous basis. And being shy, the target will generally not go to anyone and tell them about it because of their inherent shy nature.

Teasing

Teasing is a lesser form of threatening. When someone is teased they feel ashamed, shy or inadequate. When someone who is teased while already being shy the feelings are doubled if not tripled.

Criticism

When it comes to criticism people don't' like being told negative things about themselves. They don't like it that they are told that you did something wrong or you should have done it a different way. People have a tendency to believe that everything that they do is the best and only way of doing things and for someone to come in and tell them different is not acceptable.

When it comes to someone who is shy it is a hundred times worse if not more. When someone who is shy actually puts themselves out there to do something on any level that they are not accustomed to and someone comes in and criticizes what they are doing or what the outcome was that shy person will more than likely crawl back into their own world and may not attempt that or any other act that may be criticized for a long time or ever again.

When it comes to others opinions and views of them someone who is shy or not outgoing in general has a more likelihood of reading into the statements and actions of others than someone who is not so shy. So when you are dealing with someone who is shy you might want to consider what you have to say to them before you actually say it.

Difficulties With Effective Communication

When someone is shy they will have a tendency to be quiet and reframe from eye contact. When someone is shy they will tend to make gestures with their hands, eyes and other forms of body language. When you are shy you really don't talk much and as a result normal accepted forms of communication such as verbal are more difficult to express than for someone who is not shy.

Difficulty Expressing Emotions

Most of us love to laugh, cry and have a good time. When someone comes up to us they can generally tell how we are feeling. If we are having a good day they can see a smile on our faces. When we are having a bad day you can tell by the way we walk, talk, eye contact, facial expressions and many other signs. When dealing with someone who is shy it is harder to tell. They generally don't engage in conversations, eye contact, or other body language that is a sign to others about their emotional state.

For example if they are at a party and they are having a good time but are not sure of everyone in the situation they may still remain in a corner or not dance or do something that will draw attention to them.

Difficulty Making And Maintaining Friendships

We all want to be liked and make friends. When you are a child this is even more important because you need to have the social interaction that comes with natural healthy development. If you are shy and depending on the level of shyness you may not put yourself out there to introduce yourself to others in order to make friendships.

Now if you do have friends it may be difficult to maintain these friendships or if you do you may not do as much with them as you would have liked to. If you are shy and you have friend you may not like to go out with them to different places. You may have a single place that you feel comfortable at such as your house, their hours or a local location where you know you are safe and the odds of others coming into your safety circle will be low.

If your friends become bored with the same old places and events and want to do something different they may not include you or if you are included you may not want to go. If you make a habit of not integrating yourself into the social environments with your friends your friends will begin to distance themselves from you and as a result you will have less or even no friends.

Difficulty Sticking Up For Oneself

Standing up for yourself is a god given right. No one has the right to pick on you, tell you what to do or where to go. If someone doesn't like what you are doing or how you do it and start to make fun of you or treat you in a manner that you do not feel that you should be treated then you have the right to defend your stick up for yourself.

When you are shy or have shy tendencies then you will more than likely sit there and listen and take whatever verbal or physical abuse it dished out to you. These attacks against you will become more frequent until you break out of your shell and start defending yourself or someone stands up for you and takes on the situation themselves on your behalf.

When you are shy you need to know that it is not an open ticket for others behaviors against you. So when it happens you need to learn how to react.

Difficulty with Frequent Exposure to New Situations

When you are shy you will have a tendency not to be able to adjust to new situations as quickly and effectively as someone who is not shy. Somewhere deep down within yourself you will feel that you are being judged by everyone you meet and everything that you do. You will feel that people are judging you on how you walk, what you wear, how often you rub your hands together, how many times you blink your eyes.

When you are shy you will start to see things that are not there or reading into situations that events and meanings that are all within your mind.

When you enter into a new situation you are not sure of your actions or how you should act. You begin to look at people and listen in onto conversations trying to determine what is going on and if what is being said is being said about you.

When you are shy you start to become a great observer of people and situations. You quickly teach yourself to learn the social interactions of others but due to your self-conscious nature you don't have the energy or desire to join in and become social.

Depending on the level or servarity of your situation you may have a phobia of people, events or locations. As a result your social interaction will become limited to nonexistent.

Chapter Recap

In this chapter we tried to talk about children and adults in general on how they view and deal with shyness. We talked about how parents teach or impose shyness behavior onto their children. We also explored how shyness will follow a child into adulthood and beyond.

In the next chapter we will explore more about shyness and how to cope with it in different areas of your life.

Chapter Three

In the previous chapter we talked about shyness and how it generally starts in the life of someone who is shy. In the chapter before that we talked about shyness as a whole and how it affects people in general. In this chapter we will be exploring shyness on a couple more levels so that you can fully understand it and why it is a problem that most of us have and that it is something that can be overcome with the right encouragement and environment.

Shyness vs. Social Phobia

In previous chapters I touched upon and stated that there are several levels of shyness and depending on the type of shyness that you suffered from would determine if it were actually shyness or something more extreme such as Social Phobia or even Selective Museum.

First off I want to state that shyness is not a mental illness. In today's society people want to diagnose everything as a mental or psychological defect and subscribe pills, medication and even electric shock theropy. Anything and everything that they can in order to treat the symptoms instead of finding a cure. We have become a society of pop the pill and make it all better instead of sitting down and really talking to a person to find out and truly understand what the problem is and how to address it. Symptoms vs Cure.

Anyway, for right now I want to talk about two forms of Shyness. The first is general shyness and the other is Social Phobia.

Shyness

Shyness just as stated before is a condition that is something most of us will grow out of. Shyness is a condition where you are unsure of a situation and once you enter into your comfort zone you will become okay.

Social Phobia

Social Phobia is an extreme version of shyness. When someone has a social phobia they will do anything and everything to get out of a social situation. They will find a way to talk themselves out of going to work, going to a social event such as a party or if they do gain the courage to do these things they will find a way to talk themselves into leaving early or not going at all.

Someone who suffers from social phobia will suffer from panic attacks, terror sweats and freeze ups where they may black out or worse depending on the severity of the attack.

Social Phobia can cause someone to become a recluse or hermit. They will have very little interaction with society and if they do it will be on their terms and in a way that has been planned out to the moment.

For example if they need to go to the store they will go later at night or first thing in the morning when here will be very little social interaction within the store. They will have a list and a plan on where everything is located in the store that they need to get. They will plan their time in the store down to the minute and in extreme situations may leave the store without the items that they came to the store to get in the first place since something tripped their trigger and instead of dealing with the situation they decided to go back to their comfort zone even if it means going hungry or not completing the task that they set out to accomplish.

Shyness, Social Phobia, Stage Fright

In this example I am going to be talking about the differences between shyness, social phobia and a condition known as Stage Fright. Like stated before shyness is a condition where you are unsure of social situations, social phobia is a condition in which you don't want to interact with society on a large level and Stage Fright is a condition that meets somewhere in the middle.

When we are talking about stage fright it is a condition in which you in general have to deal with a lot of people and put yourself out there to be judged. Stage fright occurs when someone puts themselves out there in order to entertain or give of themselves. When someone performs for another group if it is a group of five people, ten people or thousands the anxiety that they feel is known as stage fright.

Stage Fright is a normal thing. Everyone who has ever put themselves out there to be judged or to give of themselves either through a concert, play or some other performance has experienced stage fright.

When I was in middle school I was offered the role to play Santa Clause in a school play. We were doing a reenactment of Alvin and the Chipmunks Christmas story. This is the one for those who don't remember where Alvin gets the golden harmonica and ends up helping a sick boy. If you haven't watched it you should check it out.

Anyway, in that play we reworked it and I got the role of Sana Clause. I was all dressed up and sat in a chair and had to read the story to the audience. Now to make things worse the day before the big performance I got sick and had a 103 temperature.

I was only about thirteen or so from my memory. I was in middle school which was 5 – 7th grade. I didn't really know my lines, was nervous to go out there and perform in front of the entire school and I was sicker than a dog. But I knew that

I had to do it so I mustered up my strength, came prepared with three thermos's of chicken soup and I went out there and performed.

I think it was one of the best things that I ever did. Even though I was frightened and sick I knew that it was something I had to do to build up my personal character. As I think back to that time now I don't know how my life would have changed or turned out. I may have dwelled on that moment for years and as a result not made other choices in my life that lead me to where I am now. Maybe I would have made different decisions and different choices and as a result not be living the life that I am living now.

Now I know what you are thinking, it was a stupid school play dude, get over yourself. Yes you are correct it was a school play and I am sure everyone there probably doesn't even remember it or has even thought about it in over 30 years but the fact that I am talking about it now to you in this story just proves that it was an important part or moment in my life.

When you make decisions in your life if they are big decisions or if they are small decisions each one sets a series of events in motion that will forever shape the way your life goes from that moment on. You are also probably thinking to yourself that this is getting to be really deep thought and insight for an ebook but really sit back and look at your life and see the different events in your life that you remember and think how different your life may have turned out if events have changed ever so slightly.

It really makes you think.

When it comes to events such as stage fright and other social interactions they really do help to shape your life. Each decision that you make in life helps to build your confidence, character and the way you see the world and the way the world sees you.

The Foundation for A Social Phobia

Social phobias don't happen overnight. It is a condition that starts off slowly and builds up over time. It starts out with little things such as stage fright or fear of rejection or social embarrassment. If these actions don't change they will begin to form a pattern. If you turn down an invitation to go to a party and then another and then even another you will need to ask yourself why?

Is it because you are not comfortable with the people that your friends are hanging out with? Is it because you have to go to work early the next morning? What is the reason?

In many of the books that I write I like to reference movies. I find that it is a good way for people interested in the subject can go out and watch the movie through my eyes and then take away my vision of the topic as well as form their own opinion and views on the topic.

For this book on shyness the first movie that I want you to look at and really go through is called "Yes Man" with Jim Carrey. In this movie you have the main character played by Jim Carrey avoiding his friends and any social interaction that he can. You find him in the beginning of the movie in the middle of the video store going to rent a movie. A moment later his friend calls him on the phone and Jim Carrey keeps rejecting the phone call until he finally answers.

During the course of the short conversation he tells his friend a lie that he is home when he really isn't. His friend sees him through the window of the video store and convinces him to come out and go to the bar.

At the bar they all sit down and start talking to each other. Jim Carries friend tells him that he is going to be having a bachelor's party in a week and that he wants him to come. Jim tells him that he is busy that night and his friend didn't tell him the night that it was happening. At this point in the movie Jim establishes anti-social behavior which can be interpreted by the viewer of the movie as shyness, social phobia or worse. At this moment we don't know why he doesn't want to go to the party or why he didn't want to come to the bar but in the next scene we find out.

In the next scene of the movie Jim sees his ex-girlfriend. She is out with her new boyfriend. Jim is attempting to leave the situation since he is shy and or embarrassed to be seen outside of the relationship. Soon there is an awkward situation forming and Jim makes a comment and then leaves the bar.

The Next Day

The next day you find Jim at his job at the bank. This establishes him as an intelligent individual who is in a job that he can control his environment. He is in a small space that he can control as well as deal with others on his own terms. He is surrounded by individuals that he feels from my opinion as inferior. His boss Norman is a very social individual. Totally the opposite of Jim's character. Norm likes to throw parties and social events and tries to get Jim to join in but he refuses on a consistent basis.

Jumping forward a little into the movie you see Jim sitting outside eating his lunch. From here you can still see that he is a socially isolated individual. Why doesn't he sit in the bank and eat his lunch or go out to a restaurant and eat his lunch? With his shyness or social phobia he elects to sit somewhere he is away from the world but within his comfort zone. In this part of the movie we are introduced to another character from Jim's past who for a better term is a social nuisance. He comes up to Jim and talks to him about all the adventures that he has gone through. He tells him he climbs mountains, wrestles wild animals and a bunch of other outrageous events that most of us wouldn't do ever in our lives.

Through the conversation Jim's friend tells him that he learned all this from a "Yes" Seminar. Within this seminar you are told to say "YES" to life and the opportunities that present themselves no matter how outrageous or insane they may seem.

From this point in the movie Jim agrees to show up to the seminar that they are holding. While there you see him looking at all the odd people that have shown up and in his own style avoids them. This is him showing off his social phobia or anxiety. When he takes his seat he meets up with the friend who sits beside him making Jim very uncomfortable.

Now at this point in the movie we are getting into that moment in life where you look back and say "This is where my life changes and I am not going to be shy or afraid anymore. This is where Jim confronts his fear and begins to move forward changing the events of his life hopefully for the better. As I looked back in my life at events that shaped who I am so does this shape the remainder of the movie was well as the character Jim plays in the movie.

From this point in the move the seminar starts and Jim is singled out in the crowd as the only NEW member to the seminar. When he is asked to participate he says that he is just "Auditing". The speaker tells him that he can't audit life and decides to make a covenant with Jim that he must say "YES" to every opportunity that comes his way. Now being a very impressionable person Jim takes this literally and starts to say "YES" to every event that occurs.

Now from here I will let you go and watch the movie if you haven't watched it yet. I will tell you that he gets himself into a lot of weird situations and in true Jim Carrey style gets himself out of these situations.

At the end of the story you find that Jim has found the confidence to fight for what he wants and wins the girl. From that one event in his life his entire outlook and life changed.

With someone with fear or suffers from shyness you need to look at your life and decide that this moment, this moment right now is what you need to change and move forward without being shy or suffer from social anxiety or phobias anymore. It will be the hardest thing that you will ever have to do but from this point on you need to do it in order to make yourself a better person.

In the next few chapters of the book we will be exploring different ways to confront shyness, social phobias, anxieties and other areas that you may suffer from and help you to attack them head on and fix them.

We only have one life to live and we can't live it in fear or scared of what others will think of you. There are a lot of people out there that don't like me and I don't like them. But I don't let that stop me from being who I want to be and doing what I want to do. So in the next chapter I am going to start building up your confidence and getting you ready to take on your fears and restructuring your life to be the best that it can be.

I hope that this chapter helped you and I hope you go and see the movie. I think it will really help someone who is shy or has a social phobia.

See you in the next chapter.

Chapter Four

Shyness When Meeting New People

It is something that we all have to deal with in life. We all will be meeting new people from the day that we are born to the day that we die. We will meet people on a social basis, business basis and just in general passing. No matter how much we like it, hate it or are indifference to it we all have to deal with one another on this planet.

When we meet someone new for the first time the first thing that we do is size them up. What this basically means is that we look at them and judge what type of person they are. We see if they have a kind face or an evil face, we look at them to see if they handle themselves with confidence or without. We look to see how they are dressed, what they say and what they do. No matter what the situation we have a tendency to make a judgment on someone from first impressions.

When you are a shy person you are uneasy by this assessment. You are not one to put yourself out there so when someone else comes in and judges you without knowing you it gives you a more than average feeling of uneasiness.

When you meet someone for the first time it is generally accompanied with a hand shake, nod and or a smile. When meeting someone pleasantries are exchanged such as "Hello", "Hi", or "How are you." These replies are generally acknowledged with a return handshake, nod and verbal replies such as "Nice to meet you to", "Hello", "Hi".

When meeting someone for the first time people will want to make the best impression that they can. It is said that you only get one chance to make a first impression so you want to do it right.

Making a First Impression

Making a first impression is vital to the way someone thinks of you and interacts with you in the future. If you make a good impression people will remember that throughout the course of your interaction. If you make a bad impression it will be a mark on you for the entire existence through your interaction.

If you make a good impression on someone they will speak highly of you to others. They will say things such as, "Yes, John handles himself well" or they will say something along the lines of "John has a positive attitude. You should defiantly take a look at him for that position."

On the other hand if you make a bad impression that will be the only thing that people remember. When you make a bad impression people will think that you didn't try or don't know how to carry yourself well in social situations. When you make a bad first impression people will tend to judge you on that and predict your future actions accordingly.

If you are a shy person you will more than likely have a silent or quiet mannerism. You will not have good eye contact, have a lowered toned voice, take time to come up with answers to questions and not present yourself well to an interviewer. Now this is not the truth for everyone that is shy but it is a good foundation to look at to see if you fall into that category.

If you are someone who is shy and you need to make a first impression with someone the first thing that you need to do is rehearse what you want to say. Since people who are shy have a tendency to replay things in their minds trying to predict what is going to happen is something that will come natural to some of them.

If you are going to go on an interview or take part in a social event one thing that you might want to consider doing is watching something on television or online in regards to it. For example if you are going to go to a party you might want to watch how others interact at a party. If you are going to go on a job interview then you might want to watch someone on a job interview.

The idea behind this is for you to associate yourself with the situation. If you have never been on a job interview before or if you have never been to a party before you will have no frame of reference to act off of and as a result you will become uneasy or shy in regards to what your actions should be.

Now I know you are probably thinking that this is probably super simplified and by watching a television show or a YouTube video that you can cure your problems or know how things really happen in real life. Of course not. What this will do is give you a frame of reference that you can draw off of.

So if you are at a party you will know how to approach someone and strike up a conversation. If you are on a job interview you will know how to sit up, shake someone's hand or in which tone you should speak to perspective employer. You will not find all of your answers in a television show or online but for someone who has never done anything like that it is a great place to start.

Handling Awkward Situations

Everyone at some point in their life will be faced with an awkward situation. It can be as simple as passing gas in a room of other people or with someone you are close to. You might meet up with someone you owe money to or who owes money to you or someone that you just cut all contact off with. No matter what the situation there is a point where we all feel awkward for ourselves or someone else.

Awkward Situation You Caused

During the course of our lives we will all be the stars of our own awkward moment. Even famous people have awkward moments that they have to deal with on a regular basis. Take our president of the United States Gerald Ford. Do you remember the famous video of him falling down the stairs of Air Force One? I would say that that would be an awkward moment.

Now I know that we all aren't perfect and our awkward moments won't be televised all over the world for years to come. But as regular everyday type people we all do awkward stuff. Here are some examples that you may be familiar with.

#1 – Waving At or Acknowledging Someone You Don't Know

I know that I am guilty of this one. You will be in a public place surrounded by people and then out of the corner of your eye you will see someone that you think you know. Now you want to get their attention so you start waving them on and even calling out their name. Then all of a sudden you will realize that you have no idea who that person is and try to come up with another reason why you were trying to get their attention.

#2 – Holding Open a Door When the Other Person Who Is With You Is Far Away and Has To Run To Catch the Door

Holding open a door for someone is a courtesy and should be extended out to anyone and everyone. But there are moments where it is awkward or embarrassing to hold open a door for someone who is farther away than needed. If you are with someone in a group then this will not be an embarrassing moment. If you are holding open a door for someone else you might not know it may be awkward for the person you are holding the door open for since they will have to run to catch the door.

I am not saying that you shouldn't hold the door open for people you totally should but you need to know the courtesy zone. The courtesy zone is the zone where is it time and energy suitable to do so. If someone asks you to open the door or hold it open for them then the awkward ness is diminished. If they don't ask it may be more of a annoyance than a courtesy.

#3 Replying To Someone Talking Or In The Middle Of a Conversation That Is Talking To Someone Else

This is another thing that happens to me on a regular basis. I will be sitting in the other room and my wife will be talking. When you hear only one side of the conversation it will seem like someone is talking to you when in actuality they are having a conversation with someone else. Then on the other side of the coin if you don't answer the person talking will think that you are ignoring them. So even if it may be embarrassing you should at least acknowledge the conversation even if you suffer a slight form of embarrassment.

#4 Trying To Open A Door The Opposite Way From Which It Should Open

Have you ever done that? I have. Especially with those doors that look like they should go one way but really go the other way. I feel that the most embarrassing part of the whole thing is that when this happens you are totally convinced that the door is locked and that someone is messing with you. So when this happens you start to get frustrated and start yelling for help. Once you realize that the door opens the opposite way you suddenly have a feeling of "Duhhh..."

#5 - When You Are Caught Without Your Glasses Or Contacts

I wear glasses and my eyes aren't that bad yet but they are getting there. I wear glasses all the time and when I take them off everything is blurry. Now with someone who is shy they are already self-conscious of the world and not being able to see it and those around you makes it just that much worse.

Depending on how bad your eyes are you could sit down with someone and have an entire conversation with them not realizing that you are talking to a dummy or a sack of potatoes. Now that would be embarrassing for anyone.

#6 – When You Say "You Too" When Someone Says...

Now this is something that we say on a subconscious level. For example on your birthday. Someone says "Happy Birthday" you instinctively say "Happy birthday to you too." Or something along those lines.

Another situation would be when you are at a restaurant and the server says "Enjoy your meal" and you reply with "You too." Now this is a subtle statement that we all make but for some people it will be something that they dwell on throughout the course of the birthday party or dinner.

If this ever happens to you again just shrug it off and just consider it polite behavior or etiquette and a preemptive "Happy Birthday" or "Enjoy your meal" if you will not be around to wish it to them on the actual day or event.

#7 - Telling a Joke and Forgetting the Ending

"Well there were two guys walking into a bar. One man was wearing a sombrero and the other a hula outfit. Well when they got into the bar..."

Has that ever happened to you? Have you ever wanted to tell a joke and at the end or somewhere within the joke it goes in a different direction, you miss a detail or even the punch line? Well I know it has happened to me on many occasions. When you forget the joke it can cause others to look at you funny or even laugh at you in return. This can be an embarrassing moment.

If this ever happens to you just shrug it off and try to make a funny situation out of it. Just remember you were trying to be funny in the first place so why not just go with it and finish off being funny even if it is at your own expense.

Learning to laugh at yourself and at others is a great way to come out of your shell and get over your shyness.

#8 – Reaching For Something And Coming In Contact With Another Human Being.

This is a common practice if you are not paying attention to what you are doing or if others are not paying attention to you. If you are not paying attention to what you are doing such as in a subway or on a bus you may do something as innocent as reaching for a pole on the bus and touching someone else's hand. This will give you some embarrassment and shock not only you but the person you touched. If this happens just smile and say 'Excuse Me" or "I am sorry". When you handle it this way the incident will soon be forgotten.

#9 – Saying Goodbye

Have you ever been at a party or just with someone for a period of time and then when it is time to leave you both say goodbye to each other only to realize that you are going in the same direction? Then as a result you both walk together in an awkward silence? I know I have done it. The best thing to do is just keep walking and when you do get to your departing point just say something like "Later" or something along those terms.

#10 – Walking In A Crowd Or On A Group And Accidently Swinging Your Hand To Hit Someone In A Personal Area Of The Body.

Now this can be a really embarrassing moment. Especially if you hit the other person hard in their sensitive areas. Generally when this happens you will cover your mouth and begin apologizing. Again the best way to handle this is to apologize, make sure the person is okay and laugh about it. Laughing at yourself is a great way to break the tension of the situation.

#11 – Having A Conversation In The Public Bathroom

I don't know about you but I hate having to talk to people in the bathroom. If you have ever noticed no one really talks to someone in the bathroom. Why is that? I know it doesn't look like it will be a social environment but for some reason when we walk into a bathroom we become solders in the army. We always look forward, don't say a word and feel like we are filled with shame. At least that is my impressions for guys. When it comes to women I think it is the opposite. At least from all the movies that I have seen.

#12 – Casual Conversations to Pass Awkward Situations

Have you ever been in an elevator or alone with someone you don't know for a short period of time? Common places would be in an elevator, sitting in a car, or just waiting for something to happen. When you are in this situation it is common to try to break up that awkwardness with casual conversation or chit chat.

When you are in this situation you just don't know how to act, what to say or anything. This is how someone who is shy feels on a constant basis. There is no easy solution to this issue it is just something you need to work through and make as bearable as possible.

#13 – Sending Something to the Wrong Person in a Hurry

In today's world we are in a got to have it now environment. We are constantly on the go and as a result we are in a reaction mindset than a think it through mindset.

As a result of this rush world we have a tendency to do things that you didn't think you would. For example send a text message or an e-mail to the wrong person. You might dial the wrong phone number and call someone that you didn't intend on calling. Now this has happened to many of us and it has happened to me. There was one time where I was calling a friend of mine and I called the wrong person. The person on the other end was elderly and he thought that he was talking to one of his children. It was a really awkward situation that I was trying to get out of without hurting the man's feelings but throughout the entire conversation I was trying to figure out a way to hang up. Eventually I came up with an excuse and got off the phone. It was about a 20 minute conversation and I was glad to get out of it when I did.

If you ever get into this situation try to make it right the best way you can. If you send off personal information to someone in a text or an e-mail make sure that you don't' do it in haste. Once you hit that send button you can't take it back.

#14 – Friending Your Enemy

We are living in a social world. When we get up in the morning we check our e-mail, twitter feeds and yes Facebook updates and status changes. One thing that is embarrassing is when you friend someone that you don't like by accident. When this happens you scramble to figure out how to get out of it and defriend them before they realize what has happened. The worst thing in the world is having to deal with someone you don't like or who doesn't like you.

#15 – Hug vs Handshake

Do you know needy people? I know I do. Do you know those people who are all touchy felly? How about this for a situation. You are working with a friend and for some reason they are in a weakened emotional state. During your interaction with them you put out your hand to give them a handshake goodbye and all of a sudden they jump in and give you a hug.

Now I don't know about you but I like my personal space. I don't like anyone hugging me on any level. Well maybe my girlfriend and her granddaughter but that is a totally different set of circumstances.

When someone gives you a hug they are crossing a boundary that some people don't want crossed. When this happens you have two different ways that you can react. The first way is to push the person away which will hurt their feelings and perhaps make the situation worse. The second way to handle it is to grin and bear it. No matter which direction you chose someone is not walking away happy.

#16 – You're The Punch Line

Have you ever heard a good joke before? I know I have. Do you ever remember telling the joke or story to everyone and anyone you know? Well I know I have. There are jokes that I still tell to this day. Well that is all fine and good until you tell the same joke to the person who originally told it to you.

Oops...

The sad thing is that the person that you are telling the story to won't tell you that they told it to you originally they will wait until you tell the entire story and then tell you. I guess they think that it is more entertaining or embarrassing on their end to tell you this.

If this ever happens to you, you can save faith by saying something along the lines of "Yeah, but I tell it better." It might not work but you will feel better for it.

#17 –I'm Not Touching You!

Have you ever played the "I am not touching you game? This is a game that kids play with each other to see how annoyed someone else will get. How it works is that the person will put their finger right in your face or come up close to you and say "I am not touching you."

Well this is something that will embarrass you when you are an adult. You will be sitting there having a conversation and all of a sudden you will turn around and there will be someone standing right there with their face right up on you. When this happens you are startled and make a loud noise as well as abrupt movements.

This will cause embarrassment to you since you are doing a reaction that causes everyone to focus their attention towards you.

#18 – Giving an Answer to a Question You Have No Clue About

Sometimes we think we are the smartest people in the world. We think that we have all the answers but it reality comes down to we don't really know anything about anything. When we are in school or in a meeting someone will ask a question. Now for the most part we all want to look smart and not like a smart ass. So when someone asks a question and we think we know the answer we want to answer it.

When we answer what is the embarrassing part is that we are so confident that we know what the answer is. So we build up all of our confidence and give the answer. And guess what happens. It is wrong.

When this happens we look like a know it all fool. If you think you know the answer to a question just answer it with confidence but not like a know it all. People respect you when you try to be the best that you can be but if you try to be better than everyone else that is when you start having problems.

#19 – Talking To A Customer At The Store About A Product And Finding Out That They Are Not An Employee

I know that I am guilty of this. I will be walking around a large store or even a small store at sometimes and there will be someone who is wearing the same color and type of shirt that the employees of the store wear. There will also be situations where there will be someone putting merchandise back on the shelf that looks like they are an employee.

Well what will happen is you will look around for someone to give you an answer to a question about a price, size, feature or something dealing with the product or something with the store. You will walk up to them and ask, "How much is this?" or "Does this come in a different color or style?"

The person will look at you with a funny look and say something along the lines of "I don't work here." Or if they are mean they will say something like "Do I look like I work here!"

When this happens you feel embarrassed not only for yourself but for the person you are talking to. When this happens you will want to be polite and say something to them along the lines of "I apologize. It just appeared from your actions that you were an employee. Have a nice day."

From here you can go to a service counter or find someone with a name tag that will be happy to assist you.

#20 – Thinking That There Are More Steps That There Actually Are And Falling Forward Walking Up Or Walking Down

This is one that I know we have all done at least once in our lives. You will be talking on a cell phone or carrying something that is blocking your view and all of a sudden your leg will go up and down hard. Depending on what else is going on you can have a reaction of just being startled or worse, falling flat on your face.

If no one is around then this shouldn't be too much of an embarrassment but if you are not alone the reaction can be as simple as concern for your welfare to laughter at the event from the other person.

No matter which one occurs just make sure that you are okay and move on from the situation.

#21 – Your Voice Is Scratchy or Cracked Because You Haven't Spoken Yet

We all remember the Brady Bunch episode where Bobby Brady started to lose his voice during the big singing competition. Well the same can happen to any of us on a daily basis. When we wake up our body isn't all the way functioning. We have sore joints, watery eyes and what is known as a "Frog in our Throats."

This is when we need to warm up our vocal cords. Before this happens our vice might be cracked and scratchy similar to Bobby Brady. Depending on what we are doing this can be an embarrassing event. If we are talking in front of a large crowd or in front of a loved one about some sensitive topic and it happens it can be embarrassing.

If this happens the best way to handle it is to just clear your throat to clear it of any blockages or constraints and take a drink of water. Apologize to the crowd or person you are with to reset the tone of the room or situation and continue with your statements or conversation.

#22 – Wearing the Same Outfit As Someone Else And Looking Like Twins

Sometimes this can be funny and sometimes this can be embarrassing. In a situation where it can be funny is where you wear the same outfit to a party or fun social event and people make comment that you look like twins or two peas in a pod. This can be embarrassing when you go to an event and you put a lot of effort into trying to be unique or hunting down the perfect outfit to stand out and when you get there someone else has the same outfit on. This will make you feel bad that you wasted your time and effort only to have some come with the same thing and steals your thunder.

This is generally the case with women and dresses. A woman takes great pride in their appearance and want to make sure that they stand out in a crowd. When they spend the time, money and effort to be unique and are knocked out of the water by another woman who is wearing the same outfit and looking just as nice or better than they are personal social embarrassment can occur.

Unfortunately there is no real solution to this. You will either have to go home and change or sit there and deal with the situation like an adult.

#23 – Trying To Park Your Car Into A Space That Is Just Too Small With A Lot Of Onlookers

I haven't experienced this yet personally but I have seen it happen to others. You will been a busy street or in traffic and find a parking space that looks just perfect. You will make a mad dash for that spot and try to fit your car in at all costs. Depending on the street you are on you can begin to block traffic or cause issues for other drivers. These drivers can begin hawnking their horns, yelling and screaming and causing a scene. This can be an embarrassing situation because you are trying to concentrate on the task at hand and everyone is making it as difficult for you as possible. If you are riding in the car with another person this may cause embarrassment for them as well.

The best way to resolve this situation is to attempt to be patient before you begin your maneuver to begin with. You will want to plan your actions before you take them and hopefully as a result avoid the embarrassing situations all together.

#24 – Laughing Out loud At Something That You Read Ot Saw On Television And Having Everyone Stare At You

We all love our television. I know I do. There will be times during the day I will let my mind wonder and start remembering something on a television program such as "The Big Bang Theory" or "Star Trek" that relates to an event that is going on at the moment. Sometimes these events will trigger a funny thought and I will let out a little chuckle. There will also be times that the events relate so closely that I can't but help let out a hardy belly laugh.

When this occurs people will look at you and wonder what demons are going on in your head to laugh at the situation at hand. This can also be embarrassing if you are at a solemn event like a funeral or at a key point in a wedding ceremony.

We are not always in control of our minds thoughts and actions. As we get older we will learn to control it more but even then there will just be a situation where you just can't help but to laugh. So I say just let it out, let the situation pas and move on. Just remember no one will probably remember it in a hundred years anyway.

#25 – Laughing At Something That Just Comes Across Your Mind and Everyone Thinks That You Are Talking To Voices in Your Head

In situations where our minds tend to wander we will begin to do something known as daydreaming. Daydreaming is where we recall events in our past that we want to relive or even events that we want to happen to us in the future.

We all do this, it is a way to release stress clear our minds of stress. During one of these times you may recall something slightly humorous and as a result let out a little chuckle or laugh. There may be times that you may remember something or be reminded of something funny by someone else and let out a very loud laugh.

When this happens you will attract the attention of others around you. You will encounter stares and perhaps some strange looks. When gaining this level of attention you may be embarrassed.

The best way to deal with this situation is to laugh it off and move on with your business. People will either ask you what was so funny or just turn back to their tasks at hand and let the event pass.

#26 – Singing or Talking To Yourself To Music Or A Conversation That You Are Listening To Through Your IPad Or Mp3 Player

Back in the day when we walked around talking and singing to ourselves we were considered crazy or mentally unbalanced. In today's society it has become the norm. with Bluetooth technology, mp3 players, and other small devices that we can put in our ears nowadays it appears that ware are having conversations with ourselves.

What was once considered crazy has now become standard. Makes you think sometimes. Well before it became standard if you were to talk to yourself on a cell phone or jam out with your favorite tune from your hidden ear piece it would be embarrassing. People would think that you are nuts or just acting out.

It is amazing how just a few years and a change in mindset can help with shyness or embarrassment in these situations.

#27 –Being In Line Trying To Use a Credit Card or Pass Card And It Not Working And Everyone Starting To Get Annoyed At The Delay

I know that this has happened to everybody. You will be at the grocery store or at another store on a busy Saturday morning and have a cart full of product. You will get your total for your purchases and when you run your card it comes up with insufficient funds, declined or just won't read. Now in general this wouldn't be too bad you would just return some items and hopefully get your card to work. But if it is a busy day and there is a line behind you the feeling of stress and annoyance can soon overcome you. There will be people behind you getting angry and upset. They will start to give you dirty looks or even make comments that mask their own frustrations.

The same thing comes into play when in different situations. You can be in line at a train station, atm or anywhere electronics can cause you issues in public.

#28 – Someone Calls You're Name But You Are Not Sure If It Is You They Are Calling Out Because Their Is Someone Or Several Someone's In The Room With Your Name

"Hey John!" As the voice echoes throughout the room you look around to see who is calling you. A moment later you see that someone else in the room has your same name. You will be embarrassed if you try to acknowledge the situation when you are in a public setting.

#29 – Telling Someone To "Have Fun" Or "Okay, Have A Good Time When Going To Somewhere Sad Like A Hospital Or Funeral

"Well bob I need to go see George in the hospital. The doctors are saying that he might not make it through the night."

"Oh I am sorry to hear that."

"Yeah, well I will see you when I get back."

"Okay, have fun."

Now if you had that conversation don't you think you would feel embarrassed? It is a common go to response that people would give to this situation of someone leaving for an event. The event may be one of sorrow or it may be one of joy but the results are the same, you are leaving. When you leave it is just an instinct to say "Have fun."

When this happens you should shrug it off mostly because since it is such a common response most of us won't even remember saying it or hopefully hearing it.

#30 – Rocking Out With Your Friends To A Song And Singing The Wrong Lyrics

We all love our tunes. I like country and classic rock myself. One thing that I like to do is sing the songs in my head and even let a few cords out for others to hear. If you are out singing with your friends and you hear a cool song but don't know the words you shouldn't really be too loud. If you do decide to become the next Clay Akin or Ruben Studers you should make sure that you know the words.

Chapter Recap

In this chapter we talked about 30 social situations that may cause you embarrassment and for a shy person cause you to be more shy or embarrassed. The best thing I can tell you when it comes to these situations is the kind of just let it happen and don't sweat over it. We all need to learn to laugh at ourselves and let life happen.

Chapter Five

In the previous chapter we talked about different situations that you might find yourself in and how to deal with them. In this chapter we will expand on that concept but focus more on social situations that you might find yourself in.

#1 – Fear

Fear is the most powerful thing in the world that we allow to hinder us form doing what we want to do in life. We fear what others think of us in the moment and what they might think of us in the future. One major fear that we don't think about or at least don't disclose to others is the fear of how we will like ourselves after we do what we are afraid of.

When we do something we are shy and embarrassed about what we did. We wonder if we made the right decision or if we should have done things differently. We have a tendency to second guess ourselves and fight ourselves over it for the rest of our lives.

When you look back at your life what do you fear? What do you regret doing in your life that you wish you hadn't? What do you regret not doing in your life? Dealing with fear is a key trigger in shy behavior. To overcome fear is to overcome shyness.

The way to overcome fear is to face it head on. Fear is powered by our emotions and our belief of the unknown. When we have a fear we just don't get over it in an instant. Fear is something that stays with us for a long time if not for a lifetime. In most cases of our lives we don't show fear to others. Fear hides in the shadows where it grows and whispers in our ears telling us things. Fear tells us that we will get hurt, or laughed at or even worse, die from our actions or inactions. Fear is like a spark that soon consumes you and your soul for food.

The way to defeat fear is to face it head on and tell it no. The way to do this is to close you eyes and say to yourself, "All I have to fear is fear itself." Put a face to fear. Put a body, mind, and soul. Transform fear into something that you can see and touch. Once you have a physical form for fear you can hurt it just as if you were to hurt someone else.

Don't let fear grow your shyness or anxieties. It can be defeated and defeated easily. Just face it.

#2 – Keep Your Prespective And Don't Waiver From Your Goals

When dealing with shyness and other disorders associated with it you need to confront it head on. You can do this by keeping everything that you do and that happens to you in perspective.

The world is a huge place but you are not in control over the entire world nor is it over you. Each of us live in a small bubble that we create for ourselves. The issue is to not have it inflate or deflate to the point that it is constricting you from doing what you want or need to do or get so big that it gets away from your grasps and bursts.

Each situation that we are confronted with is a new moment in life. What happened yesterday doesn't matter and what will happen tomorrow is still not written. So when dealing with perspective and specific situation take it moment by moment. Plan your activities and actions for the day, week, month, year and beyond. That is what we need to move forward in our lives. But live your life moment by moment. Take it as it comes. Don't look for things to happen, just deal with what is there before you. Once you keep things in perspective like this then there is no way for fear, shyness or whatever else you may be feeling to take control.

#3 – Don't Worry About Everything

When you are shy there is a tendency to start and worry about every little thing. You worry if your hair is not right. You worry if what you are wearing doesn't match or go together. You worry about what will happen when you get somewhere. You worry about what will happen on the way to the destination. You just worry about ever thing from the stars in the sky to the breath in your lungs.

Don't Worry...!!

The one thing that you must understand is that you don't have control over everything that goes on in the world. You can't control the actions of someone a million miles away, you can't control your neighbor. You can't even control yourself at times. If you spend your time worrying about everything you won't be spending any time on living.

Now I am as guilty as everyone else when it comes to worrying. I worry about things all the time. The difference is that I don't let it consume me. It has taken a long time, many, many years in fact to get to where I am in life and I still worry. The difference is that I have realized that you know "Shit happens."

You can be the most careful person in the world and still cut yourself shaving or cutting up food. You can be the most cautious driver and still get into an accident. You can be the cleanest most healthy living person in the world an still get sick. It is just the way the world works and that is why you just need to deal with it when it happens and let the rest of the world deal with itself.

You need to start developing a positive mindset. You need to look at yourself and the world around you and decide here and now what you are going to do, what are you going to allow to be done to yourself and use that to design your life.

If you spend as much time worrying about worrying then you are not spending anything living to live.

#4 – Don't Be a Predictor of the Future

Similar to what I stated in #3 you can't predict the future and control the events that will follow you. The reason is that you don't know what is going to happen, you don't know what others are going to do and you don't know what is going to happen to them. The world is a mystery for a reason. If we knew what was going to happen before it was going to happen noting would happen as it was going to which in classic sci-fi terms is everything happens for a reason.

We are very creative people and we have built a wondrous society that if you think of it doesn't exist anywhere else in the known and unknown universe. If you gaze up at the night sky and see all of those wondrous lights twinkling back at you and knowing that out there no one else is looking back at you or even if there were you might not ever know it. When you think of that and other wonders of the universe do you honestly think you can predict the actions or events that will happen in the future?

Just don't worry about it, what will happen will happen. Go with it!

#5 – Avoid Anticipation

We all are anxious and anticipate events that will happen. These can be going on a vacation, a fun weekend, a birthday party or other social event. When someone is shy and sometimes even when they are not anticipating an event can cause anxieties and fear.

Being anxious and excited about future events is good as well as healthy. When we are anxious we anticipate having a good time at the events that may occur. You might be meeting up with someone you haven't seen in years. You might be wearing a new outfit or showing off a prized possession you won or earned from a job well done.

When you are anticipating something not pleasant such as going into the hospital, the death of a loved one or something along those lines anticipation can be a debilitating condition. So when you have something that you are anticipating hopefully it will be a positive event that you can look forward to and not something that is negative.

#6 – Say Positive Things, Only Use Positive Language

We have a habit of saying that we can't do something or that we shouldn't do something. We have a habit of talking ourselves out of things or setting our minds up to anticipate doing the wrong things.

"I will make a fool of myself"

"They will think that I am an idiot if I make a comment on that topic"

"I am not going to ask that girl / guy out because it will just end badly anyways and I don't want to take that chance."

"They will laugh at me and talk about me behind my back at that party because of what I did at work today."

Have you ever said anything like this before? Have you let these or thoughts like them come into your mind before? I know I have and I will bet money that you have to. This doesn't mean that you are shy or that you have a social anxiety condition, it just means you are normal and sometimes let your minds get the better of you. When you are shy or have a social anxiety condition when these things enter into your head you don't know how to deal or cope with them. You take this totally normal factor in life and make it into something that it doesn't have to be.

You need to learn to level or structure your language in such a way that you don't let these thoughts dictate your actions or inactions. You will need to say like, "Who cares if they liked what I did at work today. It doesn't bother me so if it bothers them that that is their problem."

"I don't care if that girl / guy rejects me, I am going to go over there, give him / her my best line and see where the chips fall."

"I am going to dance up a storm and one day I will be dancing with the stars!"

It is when you can make comments and thoughts like this is when you can begin to master fear and shyness.

#7 Don't Give Things, Events And People Labels

When you go to a party, event or whatever you are doing don't give things a label. You need to define the social situation that you are entering. Remember that you live in your own bubble world that you create or you allow others to create for you. When dealing with these events make them your own. Live them and structure them the way that you want to. Have you ever heard the phrase "You make your own fun?" This is a very true statement. You make your own fun in life and you define the moments you live in.

If you look at an event and say that you will be making a fool of yourself or if you think that people are looking at you because of some specific thing then you will make it happen. You will begin to draw attention to yourself in a way that you don't even realize. So when you go to that next party don't say that you will not have a good time or that you don't want to go. When you are there don't say things like people will make fun of me or mention this big zit on my nose. When you start thinking about these things so will others.

#8 – Embrace Being A Nerd

"I AM A NERD AND I AM PROUD!!!" You need to embrace your inner nerd. You need to accept everything that is awkward about yourself and your situation and turn it into a positive not a negative. When you are okay with yourself then others will be okay with you as well. And if they are not okay with you then you don't need to deal with them now don't you.

We keep our own company. We choose who we want to deal with on a daily basis and who we don't. We may find ourselves in situations that we can't leave or remove the people we are with at certain points in our lives so we just need to grit our teeth and bare it.

So you need to be true to yourself, your beliefs and goals. Just embrace your inner nerd.

#9 – Don't Handicap The Game Before You Even Choose The Sport

Making up excuses why you can't, shouldn't or won't do something is a problem we all have. We will sit there and talk ourselves out of going to a move because we feel we will be out too late. We will talk ourselves out of going to dinner because it is too expensive. No matter what it is we will find a way of talking ourselves out of it.

You need to take chances and risks in life. You need to go out there and have fun and be a part of the world. I know how easy it is to say that you don't want to do something because of this or because of that. I do it all the time myself but I don't let it dictate my reality or my actions. When presented with something look at it from all angles and make an informed decision. Don't let into shyness, anxiety or other excuses.

#10 – Let It All Hang Out and Let Your Inhibitions Fly

If you are shy and don't know what people will think or do if you did something? Then why not just go out there and do it and see what happens. We allow our inhibitions to dictate our control. When someone goes crazy and dances topless on a bar we either say that they are drunk as a skunk or they have very low inhibitions. When someone wears a nun outfit to a strip club we either call them a dancer waiting to perform or someone who has very high inhibitions. Inhibitions are a good thing. They are what keeps our moral fibers intact along with our personal respect.

There are sometimes in life where having high inhibitions are a good thing and there are times when letting those inhibitions out is also a good thing. The trick is to know when to let them out, keep them in and at what level accomplish them.

When you are shy your inhibitions are too high you become too uptight and don't have any fun. If you are shy and your inhabitations are too low then you lose control because you are in an environment that you have no control over and you act out because you have a foreign substance in your body such as drugs or alcohol.

The bottom line when it comes to inhibitions learn to keep them in check. Let them out to live and keep them under lock and key when called for. Once you master them you will look at the world in a totally new light.

#11 – Do It in Moderation

When you are a shy person you may have issues doing big things such as going to parties, social events or whatever in large doses. This is fine you are not being asked to be the life of the party or the guy running through the neighborhood asked while drunk. All is asked of you is to come and have a good time.

When trying to make yourself fit in or enjoy a situation don't force yourself to do more than you fell you can. If you feel that you can only stay for an hour then stay for that hour and leave. If you feel you can stay for two hours then stay for two hours. When you are first attempting do these things start small and don't force anything. As you get more comfortable with situations then that is where you will want to start pushing yourself to do more and more.

It is not a race nor should anyone make you feel as if it were. You are in control.

#12 – *Put Your Left Foot In and Shake It All About*

Don't sit around waiting for things to happen or to be invited to join in the reindeer games. You need to take the first steps and make it happen. If you want to play a game of cards rip out the deck and start playing a game. If you want to dance, turn on the tunes and start moving your body. When you don't jump in and take the first steps someone else will and who knows they may be even more shy than you and as a result you may be playing spin the bottle or twister.

#13 – *Don't Be So Serious*

Life is a party and you need to join in. You don't need to be sitting around worrying about how you are going to pay the light bill or how you are going to get to work in the morning all the time. If you find yourself worrying or being serious about everything all the time you are missing the point of life. We are here on this planet to learn and enjoy ourselves. We have duties and responsibilities that we must meet that is true but if we are so uptight and don't let things happen that are supposed to happen naturally then we are missing the point.

A case in point. We all need to have an education. We all need to learn different things in life. Now if your child comes home from school with one D on their report card or on a test you don't need to ground them for a month. You can lighten up and recall back to when you were in school and you got a D on a test or a report card. Now if this becomes a habit or an ongoing problem of course you need to deal with it, but don't dump on your children or whoever because or your habits or beliefs. It will only result in resentment and will have no positive outcomes.

Learn to smile and laugh at the world. We all make mistakes in life and do things that people may say are wrong, stupid or just not right. Well maybe so but if you can't laugh sometimes then what is the matter with you. If you can't laugh at yourself then you need to take a serious look at yourself and ask yourself why.

#14 – *Join Conversations*

Don't at the table looking at the walls, listen to the conversation and give your two cents. Now if the conversation is of a personal nature then of course keep your nose out of it but if you are all having a light conversation about a specific topic why not join in. Maybe you can contribute something of value or at the lest learn something new.

#15 – Address Conflicts

No one wants to be the cause of a fight or a situation gone wrong. You don't want to walk up to someone and say something offensive or something that will hurt someone else's feelings. But if a conflict does arise for whatever reason you shouldn't be afraid to address it. When you are4 shy the fear of getting caught up in the middle of a conflict is something you don't' want to happen. You don't want it to happen if you are not shy either but when you are shy the thought of the consequences is almost too much. So when a conflict arises someone who is shy will tend to get out of the situation fairly quickly and unlike most of us who love a good tale won't care what happened or even revisit the situation.

#16 – The First Answer Is Usually the Correct One

Don't second guess your situations or actions. When we are in a social situation we will second guess what we want to say to another person or group of people. Do we say we like something or do we say that we don't like something. When we are shy we like to second guess everything that we say and do.

Do I go to the party or do I stay home?

Do I wear the red dress or the black dress?

Do I stay an hour or do I stay for two?

Do I eat the onion dip or do I not?

I can go on and on with all the different questions that come into one's mind. One can go nuts thinking about stuff like this. The best solution to this situation is to bite the bullet and make a choice. If it is the right or wrong choice doesn't matter. As long as you make a choice the rest of the world will work itself out around it. You don't work yourself around the world.

#17 – Focus

You don't want to let you mind go blank when you are talking to someone or in a social situation. The condition is known as clamming up. You will be talking to someone on a specific topic and then something embarrassing will happen. As a result you will lose your train of thought and as a result clam up. The embarrassment behind not knowing what to say will drive you deeper into your shyness.

When this situation happens you need to just focus on the moment. Don't let any other part of the world matter or divert you from your final objective. Focus on removing the situation that had just occurred from your mind, re-gather your thoughts and move on.

#18 – Remove Yourself from Rejection

Not everyone in the world will like what you do or what you stand for. There will be times when you put yourself out there and rejections will be placed upon you. The best thing to do is brush it off, refocus your mind and your energy and move forward.

Rejection from a Job

We all work as hard as we can and want to have our dream jobs. But for some people that might not be a possibility. If you go out there and put in applications you might be rejected for the position because of educational reasons or perhaps you don't have the skills to complete the jobs requirements.

The best way to handle this is to find out why you were rejected and to fix the situation. If you need more education and this is the field that you want to work in then you may want to find a school that teaches what you want to learn. If you need more skills to work the job see if there is someone who will apprentice you so that you can work in the field that you enjoy and gain the knowledge and experience that employers want from you. Then go back and apply again.

Rejection from a Relationship

There is someone out there for everyone you just need to look. Sometimes the journey is a long and lonely one but if you keep looking and put yourself out there then to be hurt the possibility of finding someone increases.

If you sit in the corner at a party and don't go and talk to anyone then you will probably not meet someone. If you do go up to someone and say "hi", not some made up line or some gimmick to score, just be honest with someone and then see what happens. If you do that then the possibilities for success increase. If you go up being Mr. Cool and nothing matters to you then of course people will look at you with unkempt and you will not get anywhere.

#19 – Make Friends, Don't Be Shy

Go out there and introduce yourself to others. Make people your friends. Making friends is probably one of the hardest and easiest thing to do at the same time.

To make a friend all you need to do is strike up a conversation and have a common interest. It is funny to look back at how I made friends growing up. I either made them one of three ways. The first was we had a common interest.

The second is if they were a friend with one of the friends that I already had and third if we got into a fight and slapped each other around for a while.

The worst thing that can happen is they say they don't want to be friends. And what that happens don't force the issue just go with it and find someone else to hang out with.

#20 – Build Yourself Up

You want to build yourself up to be the best person that you can be. When you look good, feel good and build confidence then the rest of the world will follow. If you make yourself out to be your best then there is no reason to be shy or self-conscious. If you feel good then who cares what others think.

Chapter Six

So far within this book we have talked about shyness and other social disorders that come along with shyness. In this chapter and the chapters that will follow we will be telling you some stories that relate to specific shyness and social disorders and their triggers. Trigger stories that we will be talking about will cover but not be limited to

- Meeting New People

- Being the Center Of Attention

I hope that you enjoy these stories and I hope that you can take something away from them that you can use in resolving your own issues with shyness.

MEETING PEOPLE

The ground was wet when he pulled into town. The rain had fallen fairly hard from the night before. As Robert drove into town the feeling of uneasiness soon overcame him. "I wonder if I had made the right decision coming here?" he thought to himself.

Robert, a young man of eighteen has decided to strike out on his own. Working all summer as a helper at his uncles Construction Company he had saved up enough money to pay rent and utilities on an apartment for six months as well as have some spending money to get himself started in his new town.

Moving from the big city of Boston Mass to the small little town Goose Creek right outside of Charleston SC, Robert was entering into new territory hopefully filled with fun and adventure. The only problem is that Robert was never a real outgoing person. Throughout most of his life he stayed to himself not really putting himself out there and making many friends. In fact you could say that Robert was shy.

As a child Robert would spend most of his time in his room playing with action figures, reading comic books and hiding himself away in his own little world. His parents tried to be supportive of their son, they encouraged him to go ond meet people, attend parties, try out for sports or other social events but Robert really didn't have any interest in those events. He just liked doing what he was doing and it seemed to fit him just fine.

Now he was entering into a brand new world. A world filled with new opportunities and challenges. Robert is now in a position where he can't really hide himself away from the world, he is forced to confront it on its terms no matter what happens.

Goose Creek was a small town for the most part. The people there are nice and the opportunity for employment was fairly plentiful. With his skills in construction it probably wouldn't be long before he found a job. But where to look?

Being a shy person Robert needs to look within himself and find his inner strength and use that to survive. The first hurdle Robert needs to overcome is meeting new people. This shouldn't be hard for him since he is in a new town and no one knows him so everyone he meets will be new. With having money in his pocket finding a job will more than likely be a secondary concern. The first order of business for him is to find somewhere to live.

When looking for a place to live Robert will have to deal with a lot of different people that he never had to deal with before. This can be a scary situation all around. Looking through the local papers and through apartment magazines he locates several that peak his interest. The first thing that Robert will have to do is call these places on the phone.

Calling on the phone isn't really a big issue with Robert since he talks on the phone all the time. But for many with a shy personality it can become an issue. Not knowing the other person on the phone can be unnerving. Picking up the phone Robert calls a nice apartment complex in the area.

"Hello"

"Yes hello, my name is Robert Perkins. I have just moved to your state and am looking for an apartment to rent. I see that you have several of them available. When would be a good time to setup an appointment to see the apartments?"

A moment of silence fills the air and then the woman on the other end of the phone continues to talk. "Well Mr. Perkins, it appears that we have an opening to do a showing at three o'clock today. Would that be a good time for you to come by and take a look at the apartment?"

"Yes, that will be a fine time to come by and check them out. Who do I ask for?"

"You can ask for me. My name is Julie."

"Okay Julie, I appreciate your time and will see you later today at three."

"Great, I will see you then."

Now that conversation doesn't seem like it would have been an issue for Richard and it wasn't. But for some people a conversation like that would have been hard to deal with. When you have an issue dealing with people because of shyness this exchange may have been a nightmare.

Driving around town for a few hours picking up on the roads and the businesses in the area Richard soon arrives at the apartment complex. Pulling his car up to the apartment office Richard gets out of the car and walks up towards the office. Richard's hands begin to sweat a little and his heart begins to beat a little faster. Reaching his hand up to open the door he hears a slight buzzing noise and the door swings open.

"Oh hello there." Came the voice of an attractive woman. "My name is Julie Montgomery."

You look at the lovely woman standing there before you with her hand out stretched greeting you as you approach. Glancing down at her hand you hesitate for a moment before mustering up the courage and strength to take her hand in yours.

"Hello," you say as your voice begins to crack slightly. "My name is Richard. I believe It talked to you about the apartment."

"Oh yes Richard." A smile fills her face. "I am glad that you have decided to come and consider our lovely complex as the site for your new home. Why don't you come on in and we can start telling you about our complex."

"That sounds great."

Stepping aside Julie turns around and makes space for you to enter the office. You quickly walk through the door and enter the office. As you look around you can see that it is well decorated. There are some palm trees decorating the lobby area as well as s pineapple, actually several pineapples adorning the walls and other areas of the room as decoration.

As you follow Julie through the office you notice one or two other people sitting at desks, talking on phones and even one standing outside in the courtyard smoking a cigarette. Turning a small corner you enter a smaller office where you are offered a place to sit.

"Well Richard," she motions to the chair, "Why don't you take a seat and we can chat."

Moving to one of the leather bound chairs Richard takes a deep breath and sits in one of the chairs. "Why don't you tell me about yourself."

An uneasy feeling washes over you as you begin to muster up the strength to talk. Ever since you were a kid you didn't like talking about yourself and what you liked to do and how you liked to do it. Those feelings have gotten better over the years but as a whole you still have stage fright when it comes to talking in public.

Closing your eyes for a moment and taking a deep breath you count to ten and begin to speak.

"Well, I am eighteen years old and I moved down here from New York. I am in the construction field and decided to come down here to the lovely state of South Carolina to enjoy southern hospitality and the warm weather. Those winters in New York are starting to get to me."

"I can imagine." Stated jullie. "What type of job do you have down here and how do you plan to be able to make rent?" The interview process went on for about another twenty minutes and after checking out a few apartments decides to take one.

Success. Richard overcame his fear of dealing with people in a social situation. The first step has been achieved, now onto the next one. Moving in and meeting other tenants.

Getting an apartment or other things that people want when they are shy can be a challenge. When they have to deal with people on a social level their fear and anxiety can grow to dangerous levels. Richard handled it fairly well but his journey is not yet over.

With keys in hand and a sense of pride and commitment Richard makes his way to his apartment for the first time. Getting out of his car he walks down the side walk and through the archway and towards his apartment. Looking at the numbers on the doors he finds his apartment number five.

Taking his key in his hand he unlocks the door and walks in. The apartment is like all the others in the complex. A two bedroom one bath unit with kitchen and washer dryer connections. Walking out onto the outside deck Richard sees another tenant sitting on his porch drinking a beer.

Getting up from his chair when he notices Richard the man walks over to his railing which is only about five feet away from Richards and introduces himself. With his hand outstretched to shake your hand the man introduces himself to Richard,

"Hello buddy I see you are moving in to the complex. My name is Stephen but everyone around here calls me Mr. D."

Hesitating for a moment Richard takes another deep breath, looks the main in the face and replies back. "Hello Stephen, my name is Richard. Nice to meet you." The two men strike up a conversation for a few minutes before Stephen is called away by his wife to take care of a few things in the apartment.

Second hurdle overcome.

As Richard walks back into the apartment the feeling of shyness seem to be diminishing with each new encounter. If this cycle continues then perhaps he can overcome his shyness all together. Only time will tell.

We will leave Richard to explore South Carolina and his new environment in more detail. From the story that I told you so far you can see how one can deal with shyness and social situations. Richard's situation is like all of our situations. He had to deal with his fears and put himself in a situation where he had no choice but to deal with them.

If you deal with issues like Richards you need to follow his example. Put yourself into a situation where you need to deal with your fears. You need to break yourself out of your comfort zone and take actions to make your life a better one.

In the next story I will talk about being the center of attention. Come join us.

Center Of Attention

Being the center of attention can be a very good thing or it can be a very bad thing. In this story I am going to talk about how my friend Chris became the center of attention one day at school.

It was back in about tenth grade and we were all retting ready to play a game of kickball outside. Now I hated gym with a passion and just wanted to go back to working on the computer or doing something that I enjoyed doing instead of running around a nasty field playing with a ball.

Anyway I had a friend named Chris and he was like me. He didn't like to go out and play in Gym either but since we were kids we had no choice. Anyway that day the field was wet and muddy and there was a little bit of a chill in the air. I especially didn't want to go out and play kickball but for some reason my friend Chris wanted to go. So I bit the bullet and went for it.

The game started like any other with me and Chris being picked last for the team. What an embarrassment. I mean I have to go out there and do this crap and then have to deal with the embarrassment of being picked last. I just wanted to go home.

As I looked at my friend Chris I noticed that he was smiling and actually excited to play. I walked over to him and asked him what was going on. He looked at me and started to tell me about this girl that he was interested in called Donna.

He pointed around to the bleachers where several of the other students were sitting watching the game on their study hall period.

"Do you see the girl in the white sweater?" he asked.

I looked over to the bleachers and saw a tall girl in a white sweater sitting with some of her friends. The girl was cute. She had long blonde hair, blue eyes and a cute smile. I looked back at Chris and then back at Donna. For a moment the two were smiling at each other like some sick puppy love.

Chris leaned over towards me and spoke.

"Dude, I need you to totally hook me up today."

Looking back at him with a blank expression I pondered what he was talking about. "What do you mean by hooking you up?" The question hung there in the air for what seemed like a minute before he replied.

"I need you to do an amazing kick to me so I can dive for the ball, catch it and look really cool in front f Donna." As each word passed through his lips his eyes never left their gaze of the girl sitting in the bleachers.

"I don't know. You know I can't play this stupid stuff."

Slapping me on the shoulders he turned his gaze from Donna and placed it towards me. "I know you can do it. Listen, I will give you a signal and when I do I want you to kick the ball as hard as you can into the air so that I can do my thing, catch it and be a hero. I know I can count on you."

With another quick slap on the back the Gym teacher blew his whistle and Chris gave me a waving signal indicating to me that this was what he wanted me to use as his signal as he ran across the field to his position.

"What in the world did I get myself into?" I thought as I made my way across the field.

The game started and we quickly went into action. The ground was slick and wet but we were still able to keep our footing throughout the game. As we continued to play a grumble of thunder echoed in the distance.

The whistle blew from the gym teacher's lips as he announced that this was going to be our last play of the game before we packed it up and had to head out. Chris looked at me with the signal and as if I didn't already know that this was going to be the play of the game. I took a deep breath as I took my position to perform this stupid play and waited for the whistle to blow.

"SSSSHHHHHHHHH" Went the sound of the whistle. We quickly all ascend on the ball but I got to it first and quickly knocked it into the air. A moment later all I remember hearing was a loud thump and a huge eruption of laughter.

When I turned around to see what everyone was laughing at all I could see was Chris running away from the field with his paints around his ankles. Apparently when he went up and caught the ball his paints were loose and they fell down.

Looking over at the bleacher I could see Donna as well as the other girls laughing hysterically at what has happened. A moment passes I look around and see that Chris is nowhere to be seen. Taking in the entire situation I can't imagine the humiliation that Chris felt from the situation.

After a few days of teasing and some joking around at his expense everything died down from that incident but I still think that the events of that day stay with him. As far as him and Donna go they are happily married after twenty years. They have two boys Nicki and Alex and are expecting their first granddaughter next spring.

I guess he impressed her after all.

Diary Of A Shy Girl

January 15th

My name is not important but my story is. I don't expect anyone to read this but me and my cat curious. It is hard for me to talk to others be it my mom, dad or even my friends how few I actually have. I don't know what is wrong with me. I want to have friends, I want others to like me but I guess I am just shy.

I feel better writing down my thoughts. The words seem to flow better from my pen than they do from my lips. All I can say about myself is that I am a teenage girl wanting to be accepted into this world, find love and return love in exchange.

Through these pages I hope to find the confidence that I am lacking and hope to one day be rid of this illness I call shyness. It will be my dream to one day have a child of my own and teach her all about the wonders of this great world.

From these pages I hope that you learn to understand me and one day love me. But what to do from here?

January 22nd

From my room today I saw a bird sitting on a tree branch outside my window. Its songs filled my heart with joy. It is said that it will snow tomorrow. I am hoping that it does and school is shut down. I have been enjoying my weekend away from all the other students. I like them and all but for some reason I just can't talk to any of them.

I walk the halls of my school with my books up on my chest and my head down. I can hear all the other students whispering behind my back about me. They say I am stuck up and I come from a rich family. I don't know why they think that they can judge me without even knowing me.

I agree that I haven't made it easy for any of them to get to know me but none have even tried either. I feel that there is something wrong with me. I can't put my finger on it I just have some condition in me that I just can't explain.

I just wish for it to snow tomorrow so I don't have to face the other kids.

January 23rd

No luck today with the snow day. I had to go to school. There was a bitter wind blowing outside though, it made me shiver throughout my body. For once I had a reason to burry my face down away from others glances and glares.

There was a bright spot in the day today. We had a new student come to class. His name was Eric and he was so cute. He had long flowing blonde hair and blue eyes that just shimmed and sparkled like nothing I had ever seen before.

Ahhh..

I don't know why I am dreaming about him, noting will ever happen. I just don't know how to talk to him or to anyone for that matter. I am such a loser. I wish I just knew what was wrong.

January 25th

I am such a dork. I can't believe what happened today. If I could find a hole big enough I would just crawl up and die!

Today in school I was sitting in the lunch room and my friend Leslie came over to me and started talking. Leslie and I have been friends since we were three years old. She is the only one that I feel comfortable talking to about things that go on in my life.

Anyway during lunch today she came up to me and told me that some of the guys were talking and they told her that the new guy Eric thought I was cute. Me cute. I don't think so. I mean I am not a dog by any means but I don't think that I am cute.

Now that isn't really the bad part. The bad part is that she told me that they waned me to go to a party this weekend so that we could all get to know each other better.

A party, I could just die. I haven't been to a party in years. The last time I went to a party I think I was like twelve years old and it was Leslie's birthday party. From what I can remember from that experience that the party didn't end well. I recall drinking a lot of punch and throwing up on some clowns shoes.

Now I am going to go to another party. I don't think that I can handle it. I want to go but with all those people looking at me and then on top of that to talk to a cute guy.

I just want to crawl up into a ball and die.

January 26th

"OH MY GOD!!"

Today was a good day. Well I think it was a good day. I actually had the nerves to talk to Eric. I mean, I, I just can't put it into words.

Okay, like, I was walking to my locker before second period and I could feel someone walking up behind me. I was just about to turn around when I heard a boys voice speaking to me. I slowly turned my head around and saw that it was Eric.

"Hi" he said, "My name is Eric."

I stood there speechless. I wanted to run away and hide but for some reason my feet were glued into place. He looked at me with this amazing smile and all I could do was sit there attempting not to let drool hit my shoes.

Moments later he spoke again and started to tell me that he was new to the school and wanted to get to know me. He started saying other stuff as well but I was so nervous and awestruck that I just couldn't even concentrate on what he was saying.

The only thing I can recall was that he was looking forward to seeing me at his house for a party that weekend. The last thing I can remember him saying was "You'll be there right?"

And all I can remember saying was "uhun"

Then he walked away.

It took me a minute to get myself back together but when I did I realized that I talked to a boy. Oh my god! I talked to a boy!

January 29th

It is only a few more days before I have to go to this party and I am starting to go nuts. I am having trouble sleeping and eating. My nerves are causing me to shake like a leaf and I am torn between being excited to go to this party and swatting bullets over the prospect.

Another thing is that I am not sure what I am going to wear to this party. I don't really have any money to get something new to wear and the stuff I do have is so outdated. I fear if I go to this party wearing the same old stuff they are going to judge me or think I am more of a loser than I feel that I am.

Oh what to do?

January 30th

Oh boy.. two more days before this party. I was talking with Leslie today right before class and she was telling me that Eric had hired a band. A band means dancing and I am so nervous about dancing. I have three left feet and a tail! I mean really. I watch these people dancing and singing on television all the time and I am just amazed of their talent and their willingness to put themselves out there.

When I see people dancing I see them being so graceful and smooth. When I look at myself dancing all I see is an awkward girl with two left feet, a tail and the coordination of a gorilla with a dinosaur tail.

You know my mom always tells me that I am beautiful but that is what moms are supposed to say. I don't know. I guess I put myself down too much. I really need to find some motivation or direction in life. I am a teenager and I need to be going out there and having fun. Maybe this party will be a way for me to do this.

The next question that I have is what to wear?

January 31st

Well the crisis continues. I have been all over the place looking for just the right outfit but of course I can't find anything that will do me justice. My mom said that if it were t get me out of my shell as she calls it she would find the money to get me a nice outfit for this party. They feel that if I were to put myself out there more maybe I would not be so moody and withdrawn.

I don't think that I am moody and withdrawn. I don't think of myself like that at all. Yes I have my problems just like everyone else but as far as moody and withdrawn I don't see it. But I am looking from inside out.

Maybe I am. I don't know. Being a teenager is so tough nowadays. Leslie is coming over in a little while maybe we can put something together. It is going to be a girl's night. Popcorn, pizza and Kevin Costner.

Dreamy....

February 1st

Oh boy...

Tonight is the party and I am so anxious. My palms are sweating and my mouth is dry. I think I see the formation of zit forming dead center on my forehead and another one on the tip of my nose. This is all I need for tonight. To be called the India Rudolf.

Last night was cool though. Leslie came over and we ate an enormous amount of popcorn and pizza, drank Mt. Dew soda and just watched movie after movie. She came over at eight last night and I don't think we went to bed till four in the morning.

I had fun. I only wish I could act like that in front of other people. Maybe with time.

1:45 February 1st

Leslie just called and she said that she wasn't feeling well. Probably too much partying for her last night. She said she doesn't know if she is going to be able to go or not. If she doesn't go then I think I will have to stay home as well. I can't go to this party alone I just can't. If I go there alone I will just freeze up and everyone will laugh at me. I can't be the joke of the school I just can't.

I am going to stay home. But if I do then everyone will be asking where I was and why I didn't come. And Eric will be upset with me as well. Oh my god, so much pressure.

3:26 February 1st

Leslie called me a few minutes ago. I was away from the phone. I haven't called her back yet I am dreading the sound of her voice echoing through the other end of the phone telling me she isn't going. I just can't handle that.. oh god, I need another shower. I am sweating too much over this.

4:15 February 1st

Well I can take a chill pill now. Leslie said that she was feeling better and she thought that she could handle a few hours at the party. Oh boy, so much pressure for something that is supposed to be fun.

The party is at 8 so I have less than 3 hours to get ready and make it to the party. Leslie is going to be picking me up at 7:15. I guess I need to get ready.

Mom found me a decent dress to wear. I like it but I don't know if anyone else will like it. I want to make a good impression on Eric. I don' want to mess it up and be a joke forever. Oh god. The pressure!

7:15 February 1st

Leslie is here. She is calming me down.

7:45 February 1st

Off to the party... here goes nothing. I am so nervous

February 2nd

The party was awesome. I am so glad that I went. I have so much to talk about I don't know where to start.

Okay, first off when Leslie came and picked me up we had a long talk in the car. We talked about what we were going to do at the party and how things might go with Eric. We talked about different stuff that helped get the party out of my mind it helped.

When we arrived at the party there were a lot of people. I think the entire school was there. As I watched the kids going in and out of the house my heart began to race and my palms began to sweat. I also started to get nauseous in my stomach. As I sat there in the car I started to feel as if I wanted to go home.

A moment before I was going to turn around and go home I looked out of the corner of my eye and saw Eric standing on his front porch. He was waving at me. I mean at me. It appeared that he really wanted me to come to the party.

I looked over at Leslie said, "I have to face my fears at some point. It might as well be now."

She looked at me and smiled. "Let's go"

I walked into the house and saw so many people walking around with drinks and eating food. The music from the band Eric hired was really rocking out the house. If I wasn't nervous before I walked into the party I was now.

Eric was standing there near me wearing a blue button down shirt and black slacks. He looked very handsome. Turning his back to me for only a moment he removed two drinks from the table besides him at the door and handed one to me and one to Leslie.

"I am glad you came." Eric said. I just stood there like a part of the wall paper.

Eric smiled and then continued to speak. "You look nervous and uneasy. You should loosen up and have a good time. We only go around once you know."

And with that he put his hand on my shoulder and looked me straight in the eye and said, "You're my special guest so my home is your home." And with that he smiled and walked into the crowd.

Looking back at Leslie we both jumped up and down as if we were school girls, oh wait, we are. Come on were going to have a good time.

And with that my shyness was relieved. I finally had some confidence to go out there and really start to be myself. I had been accepted by someone who didn't really know me, who didn't want anything from me but to be my friend. It appears that I was holding myself back with fear of the unknown.

I am looking forward to my journey entries to be more exciting now that I have friends. Looking forward I want my entries to be inspiration to others out there who have suffered from my problems.

I know that every person's issues are different and they can't and probably won't be solved like mine but I want you to know that there is hope. Read my story and learn from it.

On to my next adventure.

Making Small Talk

When you are shy you don't like to talk about a lot of things to a lot of people. When you are shy you like to keep to yourself because you are generally afraid of what others will think of you when you say or do something.

Small talk is what people generally do when they are in an awkward situation and don't want to sit and stare at each other in silence. The way small talk works is someone will say something like "It looks like it is going to rain." The other person in the situation will come up with something like "yes I think it will later today."

This exchange of small talk usually ends there or will in some cases expand out into a full blown conversation. If you find yourself in this situation you can either try to come up with something to say to the other person or you can try to avoid it. Don't be afraid to speak up and let your opinions be known. The best way to get over this problem with shyness is to put yourself out there in these situations and confront them head on.

Public Speaking

No one wants to talk in public. Putting yourself out there for the whole world to see and hear. I don't know why anyone would want to do that. I guess that there are people out there that like the spotlight and want to make themselves heard.

If you have to speak in public and you don't want to but you have no choice here are a few points that you should look into before you do it.

First – Don't fear the audience. The people in the audience are here to listen to what you have to say. They are interested in learning about the subject that you are talking about. All you have to do is go out there and pretend that they are all your friends who you have known for years. Once you get that image in your mind all you have to do next is start speaking to them as if everyone there was only one person.

For once you take a big issue such as speaking in public and trim it down into a more manageable part then the huge picture becomes the pieces and you can easily manipulate one piece of a puzzle instead of carrying the entire thing at one time.

Performing On Stage

We are not all actors and in fact most actors aren't actors. But there will be times when you need to perform on stage. Now there are many different stages that you can talk on. For example in the topic above public speaking where they speak can be considered a stage.

When most of us think of a stage we think of a big wooden platform with a curtain. Well that is a stage in the traditional sense of the word but what I am talking about here is anywhere you perform or put yourself out there for others to see and hear you.

When you do this when you are shy you are putting yourself out there more in your own mind than most other people. When you put yourself out there when you are shy you have the feeling that the world is looking at you under a microscope. They are taking everything you say, do and think and examining it under an electron microscope.

This isn't the truth at all. When you perform on stage no matter what it is made out of you are putting yourself out there to inform or entertain. Those out there are not judging you they are waiting for you to give them the entertainment or information they desire.

So if you ever have to go out there and preform for someone be it on stage acting out a scene in Hamlet or Romeo and Juliet or if you are standing on a stage talking about the new features of the products for the physical year in your business you are performing on a stage for people eager to hear what you have to say. So don't be afraid to tell them.

Talking To an Authority Figure

There are going to be times when you need to talk to someone higher up in power than you. This can be your manager, boss, police officer, lawyer, judge or even the president of the United States.

When we talk to someone in authority we have a natural tendency to be fearful of being punished. We instinctively know that this is not someone we are accustomed to talking to so our knowledge of the situation is grey.

For example if you need to talk to your manager or boss the tension of the possibility of being fired or demoted is very real. When talking to these individuals the thought of losing your job or worse is a constant feature in your mind.

Another person in authority that we are afraid to talk to are police officers. Let's face it no one wants to go to jail or prison so talking to a police officer brings those feelings up to the surface.

Then we have a judge. This is a person who holds the power of life or death, prison or freedom in the palm of his hand. One wrong word to a judge can mean serious trouble if you find them on the wrong day.

Even though all of these are valid concerns you also need to realize is that they are just people like you and me. They get up in the morning, eat breakfast, say goodbye to their loved ones and go and do a job. At the end of the day they are no different than you or me.

So if you are shy in front of an authority figure just take a deep breath and let what happens happen. I know that you can't totally erase the fear and uncertainty that you feel but remembering this one thing might make you feel better in the long run.

Being Called On In Class

If you were like me I didn't want to be called on in class. I was a smart kid and I did well in school but I just didn't want to deal with answering questions or showing that I knew the material. If you wanted to know if I understood it just give me a piece of paper with a list of questions you want to know if I know and let me answer them. I don't want to have to talk to you in class in front of all the other students.

This might be a feeling that we all have at least once in our lives. When you have to be called on in class just go with it and do the best that you can. You need to understand that you are in a learning environment and that the teachers are there doing their jobs to ensure that you as a student are prepared for the world that you are about to enter.

When it come to your turn to be called on in class make sure that you know your material and are prepared to answer any question that the teacher has for you.

The better you answer their questions the more the teacher will know that you know the material and as a result won't call on you as much or at all.

It is just a little trick to get out of being called on in class.

Going Out On A Date

I don't know about you but I didn't like asking a girl out on a date at all. I can talk to women and joke around with them and have deep conversations but when it gets to that point of asking them out on a date for some reason everything changes. It seems like it becomes more serious than it actually is.

When it comes to my experiences to asking a girl out on a date I remember only asking maybe three or four people out. I can remember my hands getting all sweaty and my heart racing. I can remember my stomach getting all knotted up and a woozy feeling coming all over my body.

Then when it came to that moment where the words were to come out of my mouth I would look towards the floor, take a deep breath and then let it out.

Then when I got my answer it seemed like all of that went away. It felt like everything was all natural again and I felt fine. Then it came the realization that asking them out was the easy part. The hardest part was actually going out on the date.

The Date

The date is just a way for the two of you to get to know each other better and to see if what you are feeling is something that can grow and build on. For the man he will want to do everything and anything to impress the girl. He will want to romance her by bringing her flowers and or a small gift. It shouldn't be anything expensive just something that she can keep as a reminder of your first night out together. It should be something that is of her interests and shows that you have been paying attention to what she has been talking about before you even asked her out on a date.

Then comes the part of going to the house and talking to the parents. This was the biggest nightmare for me personally. I didn't want to bring anyone home to see my mom since I felt that she would embarrass me. There was one time when I went to my father's company picnic and there was a cue girl in the crowd. I remember I was younger and didn't have any real experience with girls so I felt it was a good idea to go and try it out. So I walked up to her and asked her if she wanted to dance.

The girl said yes and we went out on the dance floor and started to dance.

From this day I don't even remember the girls name or if I have even asked it but I do remember my mom making a big deal out of asking out a girl. She made me feel so self-conscious that it was years before I even considered asking someone out. And even then I never told her about it just for the simple fact that I didn't want to go through that feeling again.

So back to meeting the parents. When you go and meet the parents they are usually nice to you at first just to get you to feel easy in their presence. Then once you feel comfortable the questions start. They want to know everything about you. They want to know where you grew up, what do your parents do, what do you plan to do on your date. You know all the juicy personal stuff.

Then if you make it out of the parent's interview you have to actually go out on your date. You have to do all the niceties such as open the car door for her, pull out her chair at dinner and be a complete gentlemen.

But what to do on a date?

There are so many option. You can go out to dinner but if you do that you have to talk to each other. This is good to getting to break the ice but if you have nothing to talk about then the night can drag on and on and the relationship can be doomed before it even begins.

The next thing that you can do is go to a movie. This is a good date since you don't have to worry about talking or really being in public together. I mean you are sitting in a darkened room where no one can see you so if you are shy it is the greatest place to hide.

After the date is concluded the most awkward part of the date begins. The kiss goodnight. Now I don't know where you stand on this but I think it is the most awkward part of the night. Do you kiss her, do you not. What type of kiss, how long should you kiss her? What pressure.

All I can tell you on this is to just feel it out and let her set the tone. If she wants it then you will know. If she doesn't want it then you will know.

When it comes to dating the best advice I can give you is to just go for it. If she says no then no harm no foul. If she says yes then you may end up with something totally terrific. You never know so just roll the dice and see what happens.

Good Luck Slugger!

Making Phone Calls

In today's society I don't think anyone really has a problem making a phone call. I mean we all carry them with on in our pockets and have them jammed into your ears twenty four seven. But I guess that there are people out there that still have issues talking on the phone.

When you are talking on the phone you are wondering what they are doing on the other end. You wonder who else is there with them and if they are listening in and judging you. You need to understand that if they are then who cares. Don't let the fear of what others are doing hold you back from doing what you want and need to do. Pick up that phone, pretend you are talking to someone you know, and even if you are calling someone you know just play a game in your mind. Close your eyes and just listen to their voice. Picture them standing right in front of you. If you can picture them in your mind then you can pretend that they are sitting right in front of you having the conversation.

Using Public Rest Rooms

This is a common issue with people. I don't like using public rest rooms because I know that people don't really care about other people's property. Now there are codes and guidelines that companies that offer public rest rooms have to follow. But to be on the safe side if you need to use a public rest room you will want to see if there are any cleaning supplies lying around and clean the area before you sit and use it. There are usually paper barriers that you can use to put down on the seat.

If you are someone who doesn't like to use a public rest room you are not alone. But the fact is that when you have to go you have to go and you can't run home every time this happens. So just prepare yourself for the possibilities and do what you have to do.

Eating And Drinking In Public

This one I don't really understand personally since I love to go out to restaurants. I love to go out and hang with my friends or just go out and have a quiet meal by myself. But there are people out there who are not comfortable eating or drinking in public.

One of the main factors is that they don't know who is preparing their food. They are in far of getting sick and honestly I can symphonize with them. I have gotten sick a few restaurants that I have gone to. I am not sure if it was because there was something wrong with me, with the food or with the person serving the food. But I have gotten sick and can honestly say it is a real concern.

The second or next reason why people don't like to eat or drink in public is they feel self-conscious. They won't even eat in their own homes if there are people there they are not used to or have in their homes on a regular basis. I know people like that. They will make an entire meal and wait for everyone else to finish eating and leave the kitchen before they sit down and eat.

I feel that eating should be a joyous event and something to be shared. But not all of us fell that way. So if you are someone who likes to eat in private then I support you. If you are someone who doesn't like people looking at you while you eat because you are self-conscious then I support you too but want to give you this little piece of advice. Don't' let your fears or hang-ups rob you of an enjoyable night out or time with friends and family. Most of the people that you see when you go out you will probably never see again. This is the way that I think of it when I find myself in situations like this. I am out to show myself a good time not anyone else there so go ahead and look.

Conclusion

Throughout the book we have explored shyness in all of its different aspects. We have seen that shyness can be a small issue and it can be a huge debilitating condition. We have seen that it can start from youth and move on throughout your life from being a teenager, young adult and even a parent.

We have seen that shyness can be found in the home, in public, in school and at work. There are many different stories of people who have dealt with shyness and have broken away from it and still deal with it till this day.

The only cure for shyness is to confront it head on. You need to take a stand against the causes of shyness which are low self-esteem, fear and several other emotional factors.

You need to remember that we are all here together on this planet and we all need to work together as a team. If you are shy you are not putting your best foot forward and being all you can be not only for others but for yourself.

I know that shyness can't be cured overnight nor do I believe anyone should try to do so. We all need to build ourselves up from where we are at this point in our lives and try to make our tomorrows better. Don't be afraid or what is out there. Embrace the world.

Good luck.

www.ingramcontent.com/pod-product-compliance
Lightning Source LLC
Chambersburg PA
CBHW081141290526
45795CB00006B/2323